BONDS OVER BUSINESS

A BOOK ONLY FOR DREAMERS

BONDS

OVER

BUSINESS

-   MANAS ROY

Dedication

I am really thankfull to my mother, sister, my maternal grandmother and to my aunt.

Special thanks to my dear mentor Chris Haroun.

Thank you GOD for this beautiful opportunity.

<u>INTRODUCTION & THANK YOU!</u>

Thank you for purchasing my book. In this book you will get an unique experience and you'll enjoy every part of the book. I'm grateful to you for opting for this book. In this book the various concepts of relations are explained (by relation I mean BUSINESS RELATIONS). You will definitely experience a roller coaster ride while going through this book.

If I explain this book in a quote it will be:

"Its like a dream that you hold in your hand".

The book is only about 1 simple idea, just one simple ideaaaaaaa…… and that is BONDS OVER BUSINESS OR HUMAN RELATIONS OVER BUSINESS. The most important thing in this world is relation, the relation that is shared by two human beings who are engaged in an economic activity like business. When you look at the world of business you'll hardly find any business not caring about its consumers. The customers are the king of your business, they are going to put food on your table they are the reason behind your success, they are the reason why you have a Limousine parked outside your house.

They satisfy your basic needs of food , shelter and clothing. You go out on vacations thanks to the customers who are running your business everyday, for weeks, years, decades and in some cases even for centuries. This is the policy you satisfy consumers you satisfy yourself and you earn your living.

You know there are 190 million companies in the world but we only have 2095 billionaires in the world. Why is that so?

The figure below is the current situation of the BUSINESS WORLD. There are 7 billion people in the world but we only have 2095, around 2100 Billionaires in this big, dynamic world.

Why?

Why so less?

Here's the answer to all your questions. Its really, really simple yet unnoticed by the masses.

It's simple in the above picture you can see a 2:98 ratio. In this ratio the 2095 people belong to the 2% and the rest 98% are all other businesses being run by millions of people around the world.

The top 2% consists of people like Bill Gates, Jeff Bezos, Warren Buffett, Jack Ma , Larry Page , Elon Musk and so on. So where is the difference these people do care about bonds (RELATIONS) and look where they have reached. The aforementioned public figures love making bonds and by the way making bond is their first motive rather just only talking about business. That's the reason why they are so successful and they have made a dent and not a dent but that "Historic Dent" in the universe.

They love people and people look them and admire them too.

This is nothing but just the beginning of our beautiful journey we are going to cover together. By the end of this journey you will know and admire the importance of bonds over business.

I hope you'll enjoy the journey.

God bless you all.

Thanks.

"The man who never made a mistake never learnt something new".

- Albert Einstein.

CONTENTS

<u>SECTION 1: WHAT IS THIS THING?</u>

"The journey of 1000 miles begins with one step."

-   Lao Tzu

Chapter 1 : Is this bond special?

"The people who are crazy enough to think they can change the world are the ones who do."

- Steve Jobs

What's a bond? Is it more important than product knowledge? Is it worth it?

Is it the primary factor in the success of any business?

Is it really that essential?

Can we manage and improve our bondings?

What, can we focus on bondings before trying to build a huge customer base. Similar to a fan base.

The answer to all these questions are YES.

WHY??????????????????????

Why? We have read so much about BONDS AND BONDS and what are these bonds all about. No one is so focused in bonds. People are focused in earning revenue. Profit is everything, man come on. Don't you understand this?

Bonding is ok. But profits are essential you know that.

You all might be thinking this. These thoughts are driving you crazy. Aren't they?

Yeah I understand. Great so let's keep it quite simple.

We all know Intel. It's a great computer processor company. It's the king of the market and rules the world market even today. From Apple to Microsoft to HP to Lenovo and all other brands they all trust and use the Intel core processors. You know why? Yes because it's a great Multinational company but there's something always more to it.

Intel was facing huge problems in the 1970's and 80's and one share was valued at below a dollar. You can understand what problems they were facing. Then something happened in the 1990's actually in 1994 that changed the world and Intel forever and ever. It was historic and taught the world a beautiful lesson.

It was huge and a revolutionary change that changed the world and would make Intel what it is today. Intel had Andrew Grove as its CEO and he is also the author of "Only the Paranoid Survive". So Andrew was the CEO and this year was historic.
Why?
Here's the reason.
Intel had produced and sold processors which were faulty as they showed wrong answers if it was used for too complicated calculations. So it was a huge error and it could have ended Intel once and for all.
It was like for every 1 out of 20000 thousand spreadsheets it will show a wrong calculation and that too a difference of 0.000000001.

That was the problem.

What can we do now?

It's a pressure situation, the questions that hurt your mind are what to do , how to do and for whom to do ?

These questions are quite common.

What was Andrew thinking. He was accountable for the situation.

So what would have you done? Just think you were the then CEO of Intel. What would've been your reaction?

Think about it. I know you are quite brilliant and intelligent.

So let's end the suspense. Andrew called for a press conference and said " I'm really sorry to inform you all that the core processors we made this time had a huge fault in them. We are really sorry for the inconvenience. Hope you all do understand. We are ready to exchange the processors with new one free of cost. We are very sorry for the inconvenience caused to you. Thank you". This was awesome.

Really Awesome.
How?
Why not.

He declared their processors were faulty in front of whole world. He was so honest and genuine and this did the trick.

It was a genius idea. A million dollars idea.

He gave more influence to bonds rather than products or profits. People loved the honesty and optimistic attitude of Intel Co. It just got them everything. The most important of it people believed in Intel and they were impressed by their marketing policy.

Do you remember what we learnt when we were in the Kindergartens.

The famous phrase.

"Honesty is the best policy".

Yeah. It proved effective. He used the very old policy and changed Intel once and for all.

Bonds are really important than business. Intel proved it.

Ok so let us take an assumption.

I recently thought of this concept and its known as the BBC. NO, NOT THAT WHAT YOU'RE THINKING. This BBC is different. It's called **Business Bonding Chain**. I love this concept and its hell of a great thing.

So just imagine you are a start up and you started your business a month ago. You're providing consultancy services as Accenture does.

Now one fine morning you got your first customer and you served him/ her so well that they loved your services. You should request your customers for two things 1. Please recommend us if you loved our services. At least to 2 people might be friends or family members. 2. Tell them to recommend us to their own two – two connections or family members or friends.

Slowly and slowly this chain will increase from 2 , 4 , 8 ,16 ,32 , 64, 128 ,256, 512, - 8192 because were talking about only one month. Right yes. Just think 1 customer can bring you more than 8k customers a month.

It's really terrific.
Its awesome and great. Isn't it?
If you serve one customer well and make a small request then

look at the results. It's simple sequences formula we did in high school. Its really easy. So if your services are priced at $10 and we have 5 core customers or root customers then calculate this:

8192×5= ………..

8192 × 5 × 10. It's over $400000 a month just think about it.

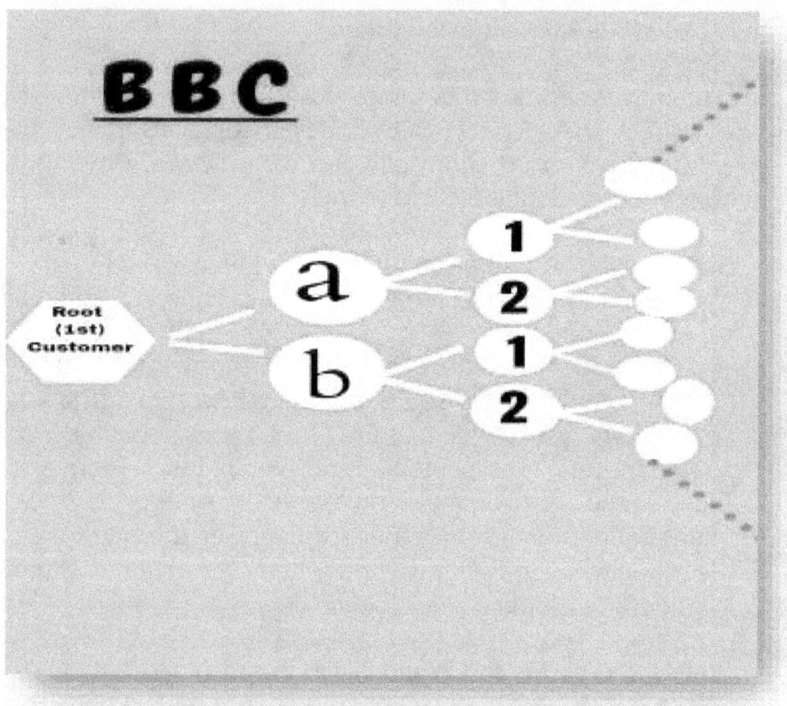

You bonded well and you got the results. Bonds are awesome source of success. It's a blessing for all of us. Ask and you shall receive.
Remember this, small things have a huge impact on the world. Change is the policy and either you bring the change or forget about it.

Keep your bonds before your business.

19

Chapter 2 : The benefits of bonding

"Faith makes all things possible and love makes all things easy."

-   Dwight Moody

Bonds are the relationship between two or more persons who are related to each other. They may be related to each other in business terms, social terms might be friends or neighbors, in biological terms brother- sister, brother- brother and millions and billions of other RELATIONS. But can you imagine a day without bonds. Its impossible.

Imagine a situation.

Something like this.

You wake up and look for your mom and luckily you see her doing yoga and you wish her like " Good morning Mom".

She says "who are you?"

Its ridiculous. Isn't it?

Sorry for the bad humour.

But let's move forward.

Here I'm going to show you how are bonds paying you sooner or later. Depending on your efforts. Some places where bonds are gonna do everything for you.

Examples:

1. Getting a job.

2. Getting a date.

3. Getting promoted

4. Getting more customers

5. Getting recommendations *

6. Getting friends

7. Getting future potential customers

---

8. Getting an investor

9. Planning for start ups

10. Gaining billions of connections online

11. Developing a multi million business together

12. X – factor *

So here were the basic examples of bonds and the results of making bonds with every possible person on this planet. There are 2 things I want you to focus on. 1. RECOMMENDATIONS. You remember in our last chapter how you learned about the BBC YEAH "OUR BBC". So, there recommendations plays the most important role and recommendations have made several companies like Alibaba, Walmart and many other companies.

The next thing is 2. X- factor it can be anything for you like for example you're a middle level manager in a company and one day you meet the CEO AND COO. Imagine the situation. This is what I call the X- factor. It's a game changer for all of us. It creates and opens up a different and unique gate of opportunities.

Indeed now there are some secrets, shhhhhhh……. Really secret benefits of making good and healthy bonds. So let's start.

1. *Leverage* : Take the most out of the situation. Be an opportunist you'll reach so high that you would have never imagined. If your bonds are strong and deep then you can take advantage of it. Like it's a simple give and take policy. You give first and you receive later. If you do something for the people who you follow in social platforms then they will definitely feel good about it. Yup, and they'll try to return the favors as soon as possible. Give and you shall receive. Just ask for a zoom

conference and they'll happily help you out. Keep going and keep bonding.

2. **_Long term_** : Be long term focused. Think for longer time periods and you'll enjoy the results one day. Warren Buffett said "The stock market is the device for transferring the money from the impatient to the patient".

Look at 10 years from now so its 2020 now and in 2030 you might have hundreds and thousands or millions of connections and remember the top CEO'S & CO FOUNDERS were made by their ability to connect with people. Bonds are great ladder to success. Keep calm and never give up.

3. **_Flexibility_**: Always be supportive with yourself. You may face difficulties initially in your career but eventually you'll get through everything. I've failed a lot of times in my wife and I love failing. You know why? Because when you fail you learn and you try something new and this gives you tons and tons of opportunities. You fall and again you get up. Again and again and finally you find the golden opportunity that ray that is too small but quite sufficient for anyone to change his / her life forever. Be flexible, adjust and succeed.

4. **_Promotions_** : There's a very good way of connecting and communicating with everyone in your company. If you are quite fortunate you can become a email official. Let me explain. Every office has a mail room and a person appointed to look after all the emails of the office. Starting from the top officials to all the middle level officials and managers they all visit this mail office sometime in a day or week. So use your brain and communicate well with the top officials and create your superb links and climb the corporate ladder or rather say take yourself to new heights everyday. "Your network is your net worth".

5. **_Back up plans_** : "Keep a backup plan as it will hold your back

when nothing is working for you".
At least have 2 options when you're working because two is better than one. Specifically when it comes to jobs. Like the current pandemic situation and the crisis created by it, has called for back up plans. You have one you survive, you don't have you starve. Unfortunately that's the ugly truth and therefore be ready with your back up plan as it is always your GOLDEN LIFELINE.

6. ***Believe and Faith*** : If your customers believe you, you're gonna do and get anything you desire. Keep your heads held high and keep serving the customers diligently and one day you'll win their faith and trust and you'll gain a huge brand equity and that's a blessing for any company. Alibaba didn't earn a dollar for the first three years but still people believed and trusted these people. Alibaba has achieved so much only because of its ability to bond and remove the difficulties of the consumers.

7. ***X- factor*** : I don't think I need to comment on this. This is the hidden part and you can get anywhere and everywhere by bonding. It creates and paves your future.

Have you ever been to a board meeting , if yes then you will definitely know that most of the discussions start with an off topic. You might be wondering what off topic?
Like a discussion might start from the CEO asking other board members whether they witnessed yesterday's soccer or basketball match. It's a great way to kick off a meeting. We all know we cannot be in a 24 hours business mode only because "ITS BEST FOR BUSINESS".

Think and act and you'll always get good results.

Chapter 3: 7 Things You should never do

"Sometimes you will never know the value of the moment, until it becomes a memory."

-   Dr Seuss

So, here are the 7 things never to do while bonding with someone whom you don't know. Might be a stranger waiting to be your friend or might be a future prospective customer.
Who knows?
Anything can happen anytime to anyone life is quite uncertain and unpredictable in certain times.
Isn't it?

Everything in this world has certain advantages as well as disadvantages and it depends on us whether we cherish the former and have pity for the latter. It always depends on your perspective and your thoughts because "you are the creator of your own destiny".
Here are the 7 things never ever to even think of while you're bonding with someone known or while you're meeting a stranger:-

1. ***Never show your ego*** : Your ego is your biggest rival. Your ego can destroy everything even the strongest of bonds in seconds. Remember how several wars and battles were fought due to highly inflated EGO'S of the different rulers. The results of which are a part of history.
Your positive attitude can create history whereas your ego can ...... forget it.
You know that.
I love giving real life examples because at the end of the day we only remember these examples so once Jeff Bezos was asked what is Google for him?
He said " Google is like a mountain, you cannot remove it but you can climb it". How interesting is that?
Isn't it?
That's a genuine answer and almost no one expected him to answer in such a way. Expecting the unexpected is what was going out there. That's a positive attitude not an ego. If you have a positive attitude you'll will make it, but if you have an ego you'll break it for yourself.

2. ***Never beat about the bush***: If you are speaking in front of 5000 people you would never like to repeat things again and again. Même ici, that means same here.
Sorry for the french but the point is no one likes to hear the same thing again and again. Avoid repeating things unless you're giving a political speech.

3. ***Don't be insensitive***: We all like something's and we get hurt by something. So don't just pressurize the other person so much as if they are in an exam and the passing score is 100. I know you do understand. Be the same all the time and don't be a selfish man only concerned with business.

4. ***Never push the customer***: Whether it's a present or a future customer don't try to oversell. If you push the customer with different offers and keep on with your boring marketing and advertising strategy the other person will just get up and will disappear forever.
Do something to pull the customer not to push the customer. Pulling the customer means giving such an offer doing something that the customer would like to do whatever you want, he /she would buy whatever you sell. That's called the Pull Skill.

5. ***Never look for quick results***: " Rome was not built in a day". Very old proverb yet very effective and goes with every business. If you look for quick results then you're short term focused and this is detrimental not only for you but also for your company. Be long term focused because "the longer the view the wiser the intentions", said Warren Buffett.

6. ***Never narrate illogical stories***: Stories are a good way of engaging your audience. But yeah... there's always a BiT LYING THERE. If you keep on narrating stories things would look like as if you're that English teacher who was known for making up stories for every situation.
Just kidding, I love all teachers they're real heroes.

When we're doing something important like finalizing a deal
narrating illogical stories would lead to one thing and i.e.
"CANCELLATION" of the deal. Be careful how to use stories and
they should have atleast some logic in them.

7. **Don't be judgemental**: If you have the habit of judging people
then you better change your mind of bonding because being a
judgemental person is hell of a bad situation.
If you judge a person just like that without even knowing him or
her just by looking at a profile picture or a status then you have a
great, great problem. Being judgemental is a great disadvantage
for your company and for you too.

Chapter4: 7 Things to do from now onwards

"Compassion is the ultimate expression of highest self"

- *Russell Simmons*

The 7 most important things you should do to create and restore your bonds are listed below. But before that let's talk about something out of the topic, remember I quoted this off topic in the previous chapter.

 However "off the topic" never means too much off topic. You know what I'm saying.
Don't you?
You all are very intelligent and smart and supportive people. Without wasting a moment further let's start the game. I've always been interested in playing and games, and the most important thing about any game is the support i.e. the fan support.

Any game exists because of the fans and without fans a game is not that interesting you do understand what I'm trying to tell you all.

Don't you?
So games and sports are very important part of our life.
I love sports you know why?

This is basically because of two reasons. A. I can play all the sports that I love. B. I enjoy every bit of it and every moment is like a decade for me. I love that moment and it becomes a good part of my sweet memories. I do hope you all love sports and are fond of some sport or the other. As far as I'm concerned I love and I'll always love cricket, soccer, boxing something like UFC, wrestling and all that. I also like guys like Roger Federer and Cristiano Ronaldo and Lionel Messi you all know them and I'm sorry if I didn't name your favourite sport or your favourite player.
I apologize from the depth of my heart.
Moreover sports are a very important part of our life and we all love sports and the reason might be different, some might like sports because of players, game methods, some might love it because of its wide appeal and millions and billions of other reasons.
But the real reason we all love sports is because it never promotes discrimination it's for everyone rich and poor, young men and old men, teenagers and middle aged people. It's for all those people who love the spirit of sports, who love the way a sport is celebrated and played.

Similarly when we bond , we never see either a young man or old man teenagers or rather middle aged man. We just bond and create a good memory for ourselves. Recently in one of social media platforms one of my friends posted something to which I commented. By the way I love sharing my thoughts on social media platforms.
I wrote that Hi ABC, You were one of the first people whom I connected with. And my friend commented " thanks for that sweet memory. God bless you".

This is how we make bonds and these bonds make us a greater person both professionally and personally.
Let's come to the point, enough of "off topic talks".

So I have gathered 7 basic thumb rules we all need to know before we ever think of bonding in our lives.
Here we have them:-

1. *Positivity*: There is a warrior inside all of us and it only follows our advice. If we think positively it thinks positively and if we think negatively it follows the same. So always start a work as if its already done. Positivity is the key. If you think you can, you can change the world. Human being can do anything, can achieve anything and can do what is impossible for all other creatures yet everything depends on our perspective. Any disease can be treated through positive attitude. Just start and you're halfway through.

2. **Rational**: It basically means to be fair and square with your dealings irrespective of the place where you're dealing.
It might be a golf club, soccer field, or even for a coffee. Relationships are always important because it creates belief and faith in your customer's mind. Have you ever thought why Coca Cola is always preferred over other soft drinks? The reason is the faith and the trust people have in Coca Cola and it's called Brand Equity. This is an intangible asset but companies can spend millions of dollars just for the sake of gaining the brand equity. It gives you a huge relative advantage over your competitors.

3. *Objectivity*: "Every action has an equal and opposite reaction".

This is what the world believes and have been believing since the beginning of time. But the funny part is that hardly anyone understands this concept. That's what the difference between the top corporate leaders and the rest of the world. There is always some objective in all our actions and therefore you should always have a particular objective while you're dealing with anyone. You can help someone or advice someone in order to win a business deal. Objectivity is very necessary to make things crystal clear. An inspiration can always come from an objective not from thinking something and doing something else.

4. *Social or somewhat not social*: I still remember I was not a social person when I was in my high school. I was never afraid of speaking I'm front of or for 1000 people but when it was a one on one conversation with someone whom I've never met or even heard of then the real fun use to begin. I faced this problem but by the grace of God and by the support of my lovely teacher I'm not afraid of speaking to anyone not even to HULK.
Yeah so you shouldn't worry about whether you're good at communicating or not what matters is if you speak from your heart then everything's gonna be fine and you'll remember this for your whole life.

5. *Transperency*: Remember how Andy Grove was crystal clear when he was talking about Intel chips and what a huge error they made while making that chips. That's called transparency. "It's great to preach but very difficult to practice". Be clear and you'll never ever... face any difficulty and problems in your life and it's not a one time affair but a life long go. Warren Buffett quoted " Honesty is a priceless quality don't expect it from cheap people". Just replace honesty with transperency and you'll win it forever.

6. *Energetic*: The charisma you have is defined by the energy you carry with yourself and that's something natural. Please be the person whom you think can change the world. Energy can change everything for you and energy is never going to be judged by the number of years you've been walking on this planet Earth. Age is just a number and I hate people who give age as a reason. Never do that. Remember this thing KFC was started by someone who was in his early 60's.

7. ***Passionate***: If you're passionate about something then nothing is impossible for you. You're God's greatest creation and you including me can do anything and everything whatever you want. Your passion will make you climb mountain, will make you innovate the world and will even inspire you to challenge the whole world. If I wasn't passionate about helping and connecting with people then I would have never ever, ever thought of writing this book.
PASSION WILL MAKE YOU MAD AND YOU'LL CHANGE THE WORLD EVERYDAY SOMEHOW, SOMEWAY AND ANYWAY.

I hope the above tips were great and you'll love all of them. If you didn't notice the above concept can be abbreviated as "PROSTEP" and you'll remember it before you ever try to meet and bond with someone new.

See you.

Chapter 5: 7 bonus point for you lovely reaaders

"Stay hungry, Stay foolish".

-   Steve Jobs

My Dear Readers,
I am delighted to inform you all that I have some more great things
for you all. I forgot something that I have some things more in the
arsenal. I mean I forgot to tell you that I have 7 more points like
the things you shouldn't do while you're bonding.
In the last chapter I showed you the 7 ways that will save you from
destroying your bonding opportunities and now only for you I have
"7 more points" to enlighten you to the skill called bonding with
people.
I hope you would enjoy this journey with me.

Thanks.

You might be wondering why did I even thought of writing this
thing in a letter like format , just for fun. If you teach someone
something good in a funny way. Then I don't thing there's a
problem.
Isn't it?

Here's the 7 points:-
1. **Don't be a jerk**: Never be a jerk. Don't just be a fool there. If
you think your foolishness can win you something it's a
totallyyyyyyy wrong concept, you'll not only lose your time but also
you'll lose the customer and his faith once and for all.
So can you put your career on the line only for the sake of being a
jerk?
No, hell no.

2. **Don't be an over smart person:** If you are too smart then it's a
huge mistake you're making and you'll always pay for that. Never
be a " PERFECT PREDICTOR " because even the top CEO'S and
CFO'S can't predict everything correctly. "If you try to be perfect
then you'll never make it".

3. **Start with small**: Small is bigger in most of the cases. The

more smaller it is the the smaller is the risk and the more you'll learn in your life.
Have you ever seen a corporation being started with 100k employees?
Is it possible?
Really?
No it's impossible because a seed never grows into a seed rather a seed rather grows into a tree.

4. ***Don't be impatient***: Was Rome build in a day?
Was Giza build in a day?
WAS APPLE FOUNDED IN A DAY?
The common answer is No. It's not possible.
Being impatient is nothing but taking yourself away from your target slowly and slowly. Never be an impatient guy as it will make a negative impression on the minds of others and you'll feel as if you're doing something quite wrong fair enough to be called a wrong decision.

5. ***Never leave a conversation incomplete***: Incomplete conversations will make your life full of confusion and misunderstanding. Open ended conversations are misleading and can therefore create catastrophic situation for you as well as for your employees. Incomplete conversations can spoil a made up deal and will defame you in your business circle.

6. ***Don't underestimate others***: I still remember when I was in high school we read a poem and in one of the poems the lines meant that "never be hesitant on taking advice even from the dumbest of persons because they too have their stories".
Never, never take someone as a dumb person and therefore never underestimate others and on the other hand don't overestimate yourself.

7. ***Don't use your jargon skills***: Jargon are the special trade terms like Debit or Credit. These terms are related to finance and

accounting. So general people will never ever be able to understand these terms. Avoid jargons during conversations. Always.

8. ***Surprise for you all***: The last but not the least is "NEVER EVER EVERRRRRRRRRR GIVE UP". Try and you'll always learn something new everyday I firmly believe that. Keep going and never look down.

 Never give up.

Section 2: REAL vs REEL

"*If you don't have passion you don't have energy and if you don't have energy you have nothing.*"

- Warren Buffett

Chapter 6: Reel VS Real

"The man who never made a mistake never learnt something new."

-   *Albert Einstein*

Welcome to the second section of the story.

I've already mentioned this to you all that never consider this book as a book, always consider it as a film where anything can happen anytime to anyone and anyhow.

That's the funny part and the most weird as well as the special content of this book.

Have you ever experienced a roller coaster ride in your life?

I have and not a single time have I not experienced the thrill and the excitement. We all know when a roller coaster ride will start and how will it end but the thrill and the suspense begins as soon as you fasten your seatbelts.

Here's from where the ride starts.

The THRILLS and the excitements are flowing like it's a out of the world experience.

Similarly this part of the book is full of surprises and entertainment and even I'm not aware what way is the flow gonna be.

Stay tuned and you'll definitely enjoy every moment of it.

I'm not bothered with the following questions and neither should you bother any of these ever.

THE MORE YOU BOTHER THESE FACTORS THE BETTER YOU RUIN YOUR CAREER.

1. What are you doing?

This means what business are you doing. Like manufacturing, selling, affiliate marketing or traditional marketing.

2. How are you doing?

This basically means how are you running your business. In what scale?

Long scale or medium scale or rather a short scale business.

Generally we all start a new venture with something little.

"Slowly and slowly we built up the nest".

Isn't it?

We all do that,

Don't we?

We are all same when it comes to risk taking?

Aren't we?

Yup we should be the same because small is always big and will always be.

The 3rd and the most important question is "Why" you do?

This is really very important for our society.

Why are we doing a business?

What's the reason for our existence and what's the trade secret.

The secret is a 8 word description.

It is "CUSTOMER". We are here because of them for them, by them and amongst them. Because we are also customers in some point of time.

In this section we will be going through the journey that embarks how real life enterpreneurs did bond and took a $0 startup to a multi billion company.

From ZERO to HERO.

This is the essence of this part of our movie.

Oooops.

Book.

See you.

Chapter 7: The Jobs Way or highway

"Every war is won before its fought."

-   Sun Tzu

"Innovation differentiates between a leader and a follower".
If you are not innovating you're not working to your extent and you don't deserve to rule the market. If you're not risking everything in all of your projects then you're not doing your job properly. If you're not imagining something that the people of this big, great, dynamic world have never imagined in their wildest of dreams then you're not living and working to the expectation of the people who made you and your garage made start up.
If you're not creating magic then you don't deserve to be in the market.
Apple Inc and the creator of it Steve Jobs believed the same and the same did he taught the world and this what defines Jobs in the best way.
"The ones who think they can change the world are the ones who really do".
Steve was, is and always will be the greatest innovator who ever stepped on this planet.
Let's start the :JOBS WAY".
Jobs started Apple with one of his friend known as Steve Wozniak, and he thought about Apple while he was driving.
Jobs knew how to bond, when to bond and how will this bond effect the working conditions and how bonds will effect Apple and its future.
Steve and Steve co - founded Apple.

Yeah ..... Steve Jobs and Steve Wozniak made Apple and therefore gifted the world another wonder.
This part is divided into 3 phases which means 3 different stories in 3 different phases.
Je pense donc je suis.
Get the meaning.

Please.

Chapter 8: Hp and Steve Jobs

"You only need to be correct once in business."

- Mark Cuban

I think therefore I am = Je pense donc je suis.
I hope you got it, didn't you?
Finally we start with the story of Jobs the most influential and innovative person of the 20th century.
One fine morning Steve Jobs was wondering how he would get the frequency counter parts. Suddenly he found a telephone directory and picked it up. I really wonder what made him do this but I think it was very much necessary to do that. He picked up the telephone directory and was looking out for something. He was a little hesitant and curious and at the same time he was driving himself crazy with floods of ideas.
He finally found the number he was looking for and took the telephone and dialled that number.................................
This wait was the most effective of waits ever.
A man picked up the telephone and who was he?
Who?
Who Who Who Who?
Was this person.
He picked up the phone and said "Hello, Whose that side?
The one who picked up the phone was none other than the owner and CEO of Hp Computer's.

Bill Hewlett.
Fortunately, it was the most commendable of efforts. Ok.... ok...... back to the scene. +××÷_÷÷£÷¥¥₩#^€÷,$^÷(#×₩*$*@€÷&$ picked up the phone and said Who is there?
Steve said " Hello Myself Steve Jobs. I was wondering whether you had some frequency counter parts. I needed them".
^=€=£$,*#¥#¥ was laughing and surprised by the confidence and excitement of Steve Jobs.
So what did that man do?
Did Jobs got what he wanted? What happened?
Steve not only got the frequency counter parts but also got a job at "hp" where he was fixing nuts and bolts at the frequency counter table of hp.
Isn't that impressive? Yes it is.

"Ask and you shall receive".
If a 12 years old boy can do something like that then why not you?
Are you different? Yes you are. But are you not great as Jobs?
Are you inferior to him or any other enterpreneur?
No, man you might be different but you're not inferior to anyone in
this world. If you believe in yourself then the world will believe you.
Let's end this chapter with something good.
"The things around you that you call your life was not created by
someone smarter than you"..........
See this video below

https://youtu.be/K_gUnEPExUo

Chapter 9: Steve and the Macintosh

"*Believe in yourself and the world will be at your feet*"

- *Swami Vivekanada*

Apple thought about launching their most advanced computer's called the Macintosh the grandfather of today's Macbook. Hope you got it right.

The Macintosh was the most advanced computer in that year. It was released in the year 1984 and on the 24th of January.

Great ...... isn't it?
But this is not about why the Macintosh failed or why did it not get that share of the market. This part is about Jobs obsession about delivering the best products to the consumer in the best manner. He gave his heart to the Macintosh. So one fine morning Jobs and his team were on the process of designing the "fonts" for their computer and the chief engineer said these 2 things.
"It was impossible to set up fonts in the software".
"And Is it necessary to put fonts in this computer? I think it's basically useless. Isn't it?
Jobs was awestruck and he looked as if this little argumentative approach by his chief engineer would turn him crazy.
Jobs said " What??????"

Are you really thinking that. Did you say that?
Do you want to say that getting that design is really impossible?
You know what, you are someone out of the world. Atleast not made for a team like Apple.
Just take yourself out of my sight once and forever and forever.
"You're fired".............
"The word impossible says itself that I'm possible". The same is what Steve Jobs believed and he bonded with people, employees and Apple customers in the same way. If someone really thinks that something is impossible for us at any time then its better to leave them aside and keep working without that person, irrespective of the worth that person bought to the team.
It would look quite unreal but that's how we should work in this big, beautiful world.
Okkkkk. So back to the topic again. Jobs was standing right in front of the engineer when Jobs fired him. One of another team members of Macintosh said to Jobs " He was our best engineer ". Jobs said "I don't care". If he is not here to create the impossible then he fairly doesn't belongs to our team".
This is how much Steve Jobs believed and cared about quality and creating that impossible thing for the people.
The process is same **"HIRE SLOWLY FIRE QUICKLY"**. It's better to do something without someone who doesn't believes in the plan of team. No one is bigger than the team. Not even the best player of the team.
See you in the next chapter.
"Think and you're half way through".
- Lao Tzu.

Chapter 10: Stay hungry, stay foolish

"The beginning is the most important part of the work"

-   Plato

Here we come to the last part of the Steve Jobs story to bond with not only the employees but also with everyone who was somehow related to Apple. So Jobs was literally fired from Apple in 1985 partly because of 2 reasons:-
1. The failure of Macintosh in 1984 which failed only due to very high prices.
2. The lack of trust of the Board of Directors on Steve Job's were the two most important reasons.
Forget that, Jobs after being fired from Apple set up for creating another wonders and soon he came up with Pixars and Next.
Pixars was brought by Apple and Jobs was again called back to Apple. He was called to overthrow someone who overthrew him in the year 1985.

John Sculley the then CEO of Apple Inc.
Jobs thought of a "Boardroom coup". A term that is very much familiar within the four walls of the boardroom.
Perhaps this means to change the board members overnight and to turn the majority into the minority. Steve did the same, he influenced and paid the other board members quite handsomely and this resulted in the change of the board members. Sculley was blown away by this and Jobs got the complete freedom to do his job properly.
That's is what he had ever wanted?
He attempted a boardroom coup and succeeded in it. He had a new set of board members all handpicked by him who would allow Jobs do anything and everything that would make Apple somewhat better than it was in the early 90's. This was the only method of having complete autonomy over Apple. Steve was back as the CEO and he had everything he wanted and that was freedom to "innovate and design something new".
Think about it, if Jobs would've lost hope then we would never have Pixars and the world's first animation movie. Pixars was later taken by Disney and now we call it Disney Pixars.
The most important thing is not the plan but it's the hope. The hope to prove to world wrong.

The hope to change everything.
The hope to a better tomorrow.

The hope to create a better world to live in. The hope to never
giving up.
The hope of ignoring everyone who thinks you can't do it.
The hope to put a dent in the universe and to create a future that
is more loveable and more innovative.
The last lesson of this chapter ....

""Stay hungry, stay foolish"".

53

Chapter 11: Alibaba is Jack Ma

"I might walk slowy, but I never look back"

-   Abraham Lincoln

Whenever you hear of Alibaba we always visualize a smart person who was the one behind Alibaba, one of the largest E- Commerce company of the world.

Jack was not the only person behind the success of Alibaba but there were a dozen more people who took, who had faith on this startup and gave everything to Alibaba.

It takes a lot of courage and tons of other skills to make a company that will change the world someday, someway and obviously in a very positive way.

"Today is tough, tomorrow will be tougher but the day after that will be beautiful". So Alibaba started of and in this part you'll get to know how Jack Ma and Alibaba used bonding and how did this bond made Jack Ma a grand fortune of over $37 billion. A boy who knew nothing about technology was neither fluent in English and had no fortune to fall upon changed the E - Commerce business forever.

This part is only for those who ever dared to dream big.

This part is for those who love to fail not once or twice but are willing to fail again and again.

This part is for those people who will try and keep trying again and

again even if they fail each time they try again.
Finally this part is for those who love their passion and are willing to do anything, work 24 hours and don't bother what the world thinks of themselves.
Keep going and never give up

Chapter 12: Learn from your mistakes

"Slowly and slowly we create the nest"

- *French Proverb*

"My life is not about what I've achieved rather its about how much I've learned and how much I've gone through". Learn from your mistakes. If a young man from China said this to someone or to a group of people 30 years ago then he would have been called crazy, freaking and stupid person. But things do change and 30 years later THE CRAZY JACK said the same thing and people call it
" Oh what a wonder ....what a smart person Jack is".
Things do change over time and people are more concerned with the outcome rather than with the idea or the process.
So let's show them the process and how things are done in the right day.

Jack Ma was 12 years old when he first found out that bonding with people would gain him a lot of things. Jack used bonding as an instrument of gaining a lot of things like.
Wait for a while everything will be fine and crystal clear.
So Ma or better known as Ma Yun was a very passionate person with his sight set on gaining tons of knowledge in the near future.
Ma used to wake up at 5 AM in the morning and used to travel miles actually 9 miles to reach a hotel where foreigner's used to stay.
The fact is why?
Was it important?
Yes, it was because he used to wake up early and reach the hotel so that he could meet the foreigners or tourists so that he could learn English. Hence learning English was his first priority at that time and he could have done anything for learning English.
The 2 reasons why he did so :-
•Jack was not familiar with English because his school was not capable of teaching English. His school was not that rich to get them an English teacher.
• Jack came from a quite humble and poor background so he could never afford an English teacher.
These factors led Jack to travel rather say cycle 9 miles everyday only for the sake of learning English from the tourists who visited Hangzhou, China at that time.
He finalized a deal with the tourists and it was Jack who would show them the famous tourists places of Hangzhou and in return they would teach him English.
Hence the so called deal was finalized and both the parties were

happy with it.
Bonds over business the world follows it and so shall you.
More to come next.

See you.

Chapter 13: First venture with bonds

"I've failed over and over and over again in my life and that is why I succeed"

Michael Jordan

Jack graduated from Hangzhou Teachers College in 1984 and he further taught in the Hangzhou Institute of Electronics and Engineering for 5 years. He worked there for a monthly salary of $10 a month. He loved teaching and this atleast gave him that push in his career that was very much required.
This also taught him why bonds were so important.
When you're a teacher you'll have to bond with your students and companions in order to grow in your professional career.
If you don't bond you'll never be a good teacher whatever you do. That's the bottom line.
So, after teaching for 5 long years Ma started his first company which was created to provide English translation and interpretation. It was formed in the year 1994 and Ma did not form it alone. He founded the company with his team. The reason is when you form a group you bond with people and that improves you both professionally and personally. So this venture was a good one but he soon left it.
A year later he went to America and saw a huge opportunity in the face of Internet. China was not that developed in Internet services whereas US was. Hence why not take the opportunity?
Jack returned to China and founded another company which made web pages for companies. This got a huge response. The government supported Jack and this business took off and it was a huge success but Jack thought of leaving it because of too much interference by the government.

" If you don't give up you still have a chance".
So did he believed and this is what happened. Alibaba saw the light of the day as Jack started Alibaba in Hangzhou with 18 members. This would change the world in the next two decades. Alibaba became one of the most worthy and valuable company not only in China but in the whole world. Your first efforts might or might not give you the desired results but if you give up then you're probably dumping your 1000's of future opportunities.
"The more I fail the more I succeed in someway or the other".
Alibaba was created to connect small businesses with their

customers. It was a model project to connect and diversify the economy and at the same time bridge the gap between small businesses and customers. These businesses had to pay a small amount of fee to get certified as sellers in Alibaba. Those businesses that wanted to expand their operations outside China and reach global customers had to pay more fees in order to get the certifications.

The basic objective of Alibaba was, is and always will be to connect buyers and sellers both professionally and personally. The aim was to create a bond and a beautiful one between the small sellers and the diversified and distributed buyers.

"Divided we fall and United we stand".

The same is applicable for most of our lives and so keep going and keep growing.

It will be great if we think this way, if Ma wouldn't have believed in the power of bonding neither Alibaba nor any of his companies would've seen the day. So think and you're half way through. The more you tend to bond and relate with people the more do you get better and better with time.

Keep bonding and keep the good work.

I know I don't need to tell you all these things but I will.

Never stop bonding with people and don't hesitate in helping someone to the best of your capacity. You help and you get helped. Ask and you shall receive and help and you shall receive help from others.

"Fools use their mouths, smart people use their brain and wise men use their heart".

Chapter 14: Jouney of 1000 miles begins with a step

"Well done is better than well said"

-   Benjamin Franklin

"The journey of 1000 miles begins with one step". - Lao Tzu
Isn't it correct?
Don't you all agree with the above statement?
Is there something stopping you?
What is your biggest fear?
Why are you afraid of something?
What was your biggest fears?
Let me guess we all are afraid of one thing, that one single thing
and that's failing. Failing again and again and again and again.
Let's relate our little situation to this one.
Jack Ma was rejected by Harvard University ten times. Ten
straight times. Have you failed this much. If yes then please let me
know.
After that Jack started several companies with his team and did
quite well with that. Finally in the year 1999 and it took 3 years for
Alibaba to earn their first dollar. They were failing again and again
and again and again but they never gave up and you too should
never ever give up. But what they gained was the customers trust
and faith, the brand equity.
That's what's most important of all.
Alibaba had a tough time initially but slowly and slowly it was
gaining the market share and eventually it captured the global
market and kept succeeding.
It teaches us something great. That is BELIEVE.
If you believe yourself then the whole world will believe you.
If you believe in your dreams the world will believe in your dreams.
If you change yourself you'll find the world is changed.
If you follow your PASSION the world will follow you and your
passion.
If you follow your dream the world will follow your dream.
The most important thing is whether or not you believe yourself
and you believe in your dreams. If you do the world is yours and
all difficulties would look easier than ever. But if you don't
then ....you know that.
Don't you?
I'm willing to fail a thousand more times than giving up. If you try
you still have chance but if you give up then your chances become
zero.
Its just the matter of one more time. If you think then please do try,
if not forget about it and keep this book somewhere so that you
don't see this again in your life.

"I've failed over and over and over again in my life and that is why I succeed". Michael Jordan.
Keep trying because you never know this might be your biggest opportunity of your life.
The Rock, one of my favorites. I love this man. So the ROCK Dwayne Johnson said "If you've got your back against the wall then you have only one way to move". You know that and that's moving forward.
Keep going on and on and on and on and on.

Chapter 15: Customers first and always first

"Price is what you get and value is what you give"

-   Winston Churchill

Bill Gates and Paul Allen started their company when Gates was in college and Paul was working. One day when Paul and Gates were together, the former showed Gates a poster of Altair 8800 computer which had the most powerful and advanced computer chips in it.

Paul said "Here's the Altair 8800".

It's happening without us. This made the ramp for Microsoft.

Bill left his studies and these two legends started Microsoft. They took their first step to change the world. Their first step to live what they loved and to do what they loved the most.

In this part I'll be walking you all through the relationship and the bond that Bill Gates made and shared with the rest of the world and with the people who loved Microsoft.

Gates was fond of computers and so was Paul so they made the most of the opportunity that they got when computers were first introduced in their school. They paid $40 for an hour of using the computer. This is where they learnt programming through trial and error method.

Slowly by slowly one creates a nest.

What Gates believed was customers satisfaction was the greatest concern for all of us. If we don't satisfy customers we will never make it to the sky.

If you satisfy customers you are basically satisfying your cash boxes.

This is how Bill Gates used to bond with people specially customers.

" If I would have been given the chance of starting all over again I would choose Network Marketing".

- Bill Gates

If you bond well you're basically clearing your path to succes. The more you bond, the more you network the more you link with different people overtime, the more are the chances of you succeeding in present as well as in future.

Bond and keep bonding forever.

Chapter 16: Keep it simple

"You already have everthing to build something that is greater than you"

- Seth Godin

"The best way to kill your competition is to partner with it". Not exactly but to some extent Bill Gates did the same and saved its competition Apple.

In the year 1997, Apple was a step away from bankruptcy when Steve Jobs returned as the new CEO of the company. Apple really needed a huge investment or else it was days away from going belly up once and for all.

Jobs approached Gates and the later agreed to help Apple Computers. Bill Gates invested $150 million in non voting shares of Apple and also provided Apple the access to use its Microsoft Office for free which was at that time the primary software computer users demanded for Mac and PC'S.

In return Apple had to drop the lawsuit against Microsoft which Steve Jobs did on Bill Gates after Gates launched Windows from the idea of Xerox.

The deal was called the " craziest deal of 1997 and might be the craziest deal the world has ever heard of". It was the first freaking time one company had helped its competitors to survive in tough times of market. It was the greatest deal and once again the ability of Steve Jobs to ask for something did the whole trick for Apple. "Ask and you shall receive ". Remember now I'm doing repetition. The way people bond and the way one competitor saves the other. The way people help and survive in this tough world.

Bill Gates not only helped Jobs and Apple but also proved to the world that relationships and Bondings are more important than money, materials, machines and product knowledge.

The ability to bond and the ability to maintain these bonds make great and successful people what they are today. I humbly believe this and that is why I decided to write a book on it.

When Gates agreed to help Jobs the latter said this " Thank you

Bill. The world will be a better place now". This catchphrase became so famous that it was taken by some of the most famous magazines of late 90' s.

Therefore Apple was back again to the top of its business and this is how a three decade old frienenimy ended with peace and prosperity on both sides.

Keep it simple for ever, in the last chapter you all came to know how Bill Gates maintained customer relationships and how much importance he gave to customer networking and other relationships.

The next part will be more interesting and full of joy rides.

" Competion brings out the best of the products and the worst out of the people".

But this was never the case with Bill Gates and Steve Jobs.

Chapter 17: Marketing by yourself and quality matters

"The best marketing strategy ever, CARE"

-   Garry Vaynerchuk

Thinking of the secrets that make great companies so great I found out 2 of certain qualities they all use it for maintaining and developing good customer relations since the day the company was founded.

Here are the two secrets and they are:-

1. Quality first

2. Marketing by yourself

Let's talk about the first point Quality first. In this part Microsoft literally dominated the computer software industry.

Why?

The answer is simple do anything but maintain your quality as its day one.

Quality always overpowers deadlines and quantity. Any business of any size of any region needs and should keep quality as its bullseye or else their days in the market will be numbered.

Bill Gates loved coding and so did his partner Paul Allen. When Microsoft was an established company in the early 90's Bill still used to look after each and every coding program inspite of having thousands of employees to look for it. At that time Gates was not required to look after each and every coding but he still did looked after each one of it.

Why?

One really really simple reason. Quality matters. I need to be sure with all the codes are of the top most quality because one fault and error can cause unimaginable and catastrophic situations for Microsoft.

He believed in this theory.

"Trust in business takes years to build,

seconds to break, and

Forever to rebuild".

This is why when you are so quality conscious your bond with the customers and with all stakeholders of your company is relatively high and it keeps on increasing and thus increases your brand equity and net worth in the market.

The second point "Marketing by yourself".

Keep the best one for the future. So this is our best point as far as Microsoft is concerned. Microsoft never had the best of marketing techniques but what they had was they were quite well aware of the basics.

Talking about Microsoft I still remember the day's when I had Accounts as one of my subjects in the high school. Whenever a

problem used to give me a lot of problems my teacher used to say
this
" Back to the basics Manas. If your basics are correct
automatically your problem would be solved".
The same was in case of Microsoft. Bill Gates believed that when
you show the customers what their problems are and you also
show them how to solve these problems and why should we solve
the problems you're giving yourself the chance of getting the
driver's seat. Here's the trick and now you operate your customers
like puppets.
You're the master.
Why?
One last reason, you identified the customers problems, you gave
them the solutions and you also identified the reasons why they
should go for the solutions. That's the only way out.
No genius marketing skills required only some sort of common
sense.
That's it.

"Marketing is always about values, people don't remember great
people or companies, what they remember is the products and
how the products changed their lives".

Chapter 18: Giving back to them

"The best way to find yourself is to loose yourself in the service of others"

-   Mahatma Gandhi

In this chapter we will be knowing how Bill Gates gave something back to the society as society had offered so much to Microsoft and Bill Gates in the early years.
" Society exists only as a mental concept, in the real world there are only individuals".
INDIVIDUALS.
- Oscar Wilde
Bill and Melinda Gates Co - founded "The Bill and Melinda Gates Foundation" in the year 2000. Exactly 20 years ago from this year. The foundation is the largest private organization in the world and the three trustees of the organization are Bill and Melinda Gates and his long time friend and mentor Warren Buffett.
The main reason why this organization was made was to relate and to bond with different people hailing from different parts of our society. It was just an effort to change the world and make it a better place to live. The efforts bore fruits and it had assets worth $46.8 billion in the year 2019.
Bonding over business.
Isn't it?
Was this example a good one for you all?
Let me guess.
Yeah.
Yes it was.
Absolutely it was a good example.
The main objective of this organization was to focus on reducing poverty, increase global education and increase the standard of living of the people in the developing countries of the world.
It has succeeded in achieving its objectives so far and I do hope it will change the world completely in the next few decades.
" One book, one pen, one teacher and one child can change the world "
- Malala Yousafzai
Education is the most advanced and most powerful of weapons which can change the way anyday and anytime and anyhow.
Education breaks down the narrow walls of struggles and illiteracy and ignorance.

The more you bond the more you connect with people. The more you connect the more you know about people. The more you know the more you communicate. The more the communication the more are the problems solved. The more problems solved the more you influence people. The more you influence people the more people follow you. The more they follow you the more and the more you solve their problems with your solutions and products and services.
Be the change you want to see in the world.

Chapter 19: No job is too small

"There is no path to happiness, happiness is a path"

-   Buddha

Whether you're a millionaire, a billionaire or a trillionaire there will always be a point in your life when you start from zero.
The journey of miles begins with one step.
Similarly the journey of millionaire's and billionaire's begins with the first dollar. That first dollar opens your account financially and technically you're now an earner. Although your earning may not be sufficient but it does matters alot. It did matter, it matters and it will always matter.

Warren Buffett was no different. It is said that if you start a part time job in your 20's then you're giving yourself a huge advantage and this habit will help you in the long run. So from a very young age Buffett started earning through selling Washington Post newspapers, golf balls, candies, Coca Cola bottles, chewing gums, stamps and several other things.
He along with one of his friend got an user pinball machine and installed it in a barber's shop. This was a great way to earn. He

got the machine for $25 in 1945 and soon they both had 3 machines in three barber shops in his locality. So this shows 2 things.
1. The ability to bond with different people like the barber and taking up several jobs. 2. The skill to identify a great business opportunity and thereby leveraging that opportunity and getting the most out of it.
The fact is that I'm not going to focus on what Buffett has acquired and what he does with finance and investing.
Why?
Why not?
What do you mean by why?
Ok My dear readers the fact is this book is not made to explain finance and accounting.
Why?
Yeah I got your point so here's the bottom line and it is that we made this book to give a different overview of bonds and the power of bondings. Hence taking the idea to a greater level. This book was an idea to enhance and encourage people to bond and make lifelong business relationships that are worthwhile.
Ok enough of these things and let's get back to the point.
So something great happened when Buffett was rejected from Harvard University and he had to go to Columbia University to persue his higher education. Warren was delighted to know that Benjamin Graham taught there. Buffett was always influenced by Graham and regarded him as his mentor for investing studies.
One day Graham was with GEICO Insurance company as he was one of the board member's so Buffett took a train to Washington D.C. to meet Graham and knocked the door of GEICO'S headquarters. A janitor opened the door and finally allowed him to come in.
There he met the Vice President of GEICO Insurance Lorimer Davidson and the two discussed finance and insurance for hours. This got Buffett a long time friend known as Davidson and the two remained friends forever and this was a great opportunity for Buffett to learn something from Davidson and Graham at the

same time.
When Lorimer Davidson was asked that how was the conversation with Buffett for him he said "In the first fifteen minutes I knew that he was a very intelligent and a clever person". That is how Warren Buffett created a new bond and that too with the Vice President of GEICO Insurance.
That's what we need to learn.
No matter how strong you are. No matter how powerful you are.
No matter how rich you are.
No matter how many skills do you possess.
No matter whether you had been feed with the silver spoon or not.
No matter how influential you are.
The only thing that matters is the ability to manage, adjust and mould yourself according to the situation. What matters is how much you can relate to other people. How are you similar to other people?
That's where you get the point. If you have one similarity then your ability to bond and to connect with different people increases and you find people who are ready to help you, teach you , guide you and even give you some advice for free.
Just look for it and you'll even find God.
Just to include a great statement from the Oracle of Omaha.
"Without passion you don't have energy and without energy you have nothing".

See you in the next chapter.
Thanks.

Chapter 20: The longer the view

"The longer the view the wiser the intention"

- *Warren Buffett*

"The longer the view the wiser the intention".

The great American sage of Omaha known as Warren Buffett quoted this.

Warren Buffet the most important person in the the investor's market. The one whose advice is considered as to be of the Oracle. The sage of Investment and acquisitions and mergers and millions of other investing policies. So in this part of our book we are going to talk about "The Investor of Wall Street", Warren Buffett.

The person who invested in most of the well known companies in the world. From Coca - Cola to Berkshire Hathaway and hundredths of other companies.

This part will show how one of the most richest man in the world and the most wealthy investor also believes in the power of bonding and making relationships.

From a very young age to this year 2020 Buffet has been a phenomenal person and a gift for the entire world. Being in the business for more than 7 decades. He has seen highs and lows from the great Depression of 1930 to the crisis of 2008 he knows everything.

I hope you will love this part and this part will bring a new phase to our book.

Remember that famous dialogue "Save the best for the future".

So let's see the next chapter.

Let's go.........

Chapter 21 : Honesty is a valuabe gift

"Keep busy because it's the best medicine available there"

-   Dale Carnegie

"Honesty is a valuable quality, don't expect it from cheap people" said the octogenarian Warren Buffett.

The man who proved that no company is safe from him in terms of getting acquired or being taken over. The one who is the most important investor of several multinationals like Coca Cola, Apple, Berkshire Hathaway and tons of other companies.
You name it and this man has got all of them in his arsenal.
That's why we call him "the Oracle of Omaha".
Believe me when I say this, the most difficult part in writing this book was to write about this octogenarian who has seen everything from the Great Depression of 1930 - the 2008 US crisis.
He knows everything and really everything. But this part is going to convey something else.
It's not about what he has acquired and how?
Rather say its about what he has done for the society as a whole.
First of all a person can bond in two ways either business bonding or social bonding. We have shown how Mr BUFFETT was a very capable person in terms of bonding with people for business or for gaining business opportunities. So he was a very capable person irrespective of the time. But.......
But, but , but..........
In this part I'll be telling how Mr. Buffett maintained good and great bonds with the society.
Before we start let's read this.
"Its not what you do, how you do but what matters is why you do.
At the end of the day we all get so many things from the society and therefore we give it all to the society when we feel it's time to say goodbye".
Take all and return it all to the society.
In 2006 Buffett pledged 83% of his wealth to the Bill and Melinda Gates Foundation. He also pledged 10 million Berkshire Hathaway B class shares worth $30.7 billion making it the highest charitable donations of Berkshire Hathaway. Buffett has been the

trustee of Bill and Melinda Gates Foundation along with Bill and
Melinda Gates. The 3 have been very influential and inspiring
enough towards the society and in removing poverty, illiteracy and
unemployment and promoting and enforcing education and that
too skill education throughput the world.
He made the Buffett Foundation which focuses on philanthropy
and several other things. Buffett declared that his kids will not
inherit all of the fortune but this is how he explains what he will do.
" I want to give my kids just enough so that they could do
anything, but not so much that they feel like doing nothing".
He was the richest man in the world in 2008 and received the
Presidential medal of Fredom from President Barack Obama.
Its not what but why you do and Buffett knew what he was doing.
He has been influential and a great figure towards the
development of charities and foundations in United States of
America.
When he announced that he will be giving a huge amount as
charity, he made a condition that either of Bill or Melinda Gates
needs to be alive in order to get the billions for their foundation.
Both Buffett and Gates signed a contact called 'GATES BUFFETT'
contract which means the top billionaires will pledge to donate
more than 50% of their fortunes for charity and donations to make
this world a better place.
This is how the richest, the most successful, the smartest of
people have one thing in common.
That is their ability to bond and relate to people both in business
world and outside business world. In society, with the people the
same people who made their products and services a successful
one.

"If you're the luckiest one percent of the humanity then you owe it
to the rest of the humanity to think about the rest ninety nine
percent".

Keep going!
Remember this....
Price is what you get value is what you give.

85

SECTION 3: THE BOND CONTINUES

Chapter 22: I love failing again and again

"If you're not failing, then you're not trying"

- Elon Musk

The 2 magical words.

If I ask you what are the 3 magical words you've ever heard you might be thinking something but I know what your response is going to be. I am well aware of all your responses. So let me clarify things for you.

It has to do nothing with love or sorry. If someone asked me the same question I would've said " I'm sorry" or "Excuse me dear".

I know I'm crazy but that's what my response would have been. Forget it.

We are not concerned with the 3 magical words instead we are concerned with the 2 magical words.

What ??????

2 magical words?

What is this now?

Why is this crazy author asking for this?

I agree that I might be crazy but I'm not stupid. If I asked something, there would've been a reason for sure.

Isn't it?

So the two magical words are.......

Harry Potter.

Yup you read that correct.

Harry Potter.

I had to include this part because it was hell of an essential thing for this book. I'm not going to include the Harry Potter story but the person who was the creator of it.

I know you all know this, the author is none other than JK Rowling. The legend that created one of the greatest children's stories and who would later be known as one of the greatest authors of 21st century.

"Happiness can be found even, in the darkest of times, if one only remembers to turn on the light".

As the quote goes let's turn on the lights to the story of J.K. Rowling and how she faced every difficulty a person could ever face in their lives.

Rowling was fascinated by writing since childhood and wrote short stories for her younger sister in the early days of her career. She was deemed to be the revolutionary author's of our time. Her works speak for herself.

So let's see that in the next chapter.

Chapter 23: The subtle art of going on

"I really don't care about money, I just want to do what I do"

- *John Galliano*

If we are talking about someone like J.K. Rowling we need a title like this. Don't we? It's a good way to start a beautiful story and this is why I thought for this early in the morning. Rowling wrote her first novel at the age of 11. Although she used to write stories but officially her career started when she was 11.

But, but, but.

There's always a "but" in such stories and we therefore need to go through the but. Rowling was rejected from Oxford University but she loved French, trés bien and went to University of Exeter. Rejected but not a quitter.

Rowling carries her grandma name and therefore she is known as J.K. ROWLING. K stands for Katherine so Joanne Katherine Rowling.

Life was never easy for her and is never going to be easy for people who tend to change the world and mould it in their own way. She had to wait for 20 years to get the breakthrough.

Rowling was 17 when she was rejected from Oxford University and hence she thought of persuading her studies in University of Exeter. She never stopped rather kept going on and on and on. She never gave up at any instance.

Life was tough for her but that's the fun and I think I should continue with it.

Rowling was 25 when her mother died she was working on Harry Potter and got this sudden blow. This was an unusual situation and it affected her to a huge extent.

She was sad, very sad, shocked and and knew nothing at that time. Therefore time passed and a year later life showed her another bad day and she suffered another blow. She had a miscarriage in 1991 and this was detrimental and therefore was a hard time for her. Time was not that good for her family life and two years later she got divorced and she was really going through tough times. She underwent depression. We are all aware of the fact that depression can literally kill a person 100 times a day yet the person will be alive for the world.

That's really terrible 

Really, really terrible. God forbid such situations.

I pray that no one should ever face depression in their worst of times.
She had a child and life was literally tough for her being a single mother. She was getting rejected over and over and over again and this was a huge disappointment for her. She was dependent on welfare scheme and things were not going the way as they had been planned.
Life was really, really tough and terrible for her.
She showed her work to different publishers and they never liked it. They just rejected it. In 1995 she was 30, she was done with her life and the difficulties she was facing. This is the most pathetic time for anyone whoever is going through it. Sometimes we all do say this.
"Man I'm done with this".
"I'm frustrated with this.
I can't take this anymore".
So Rowling wanted to commit suicide. But she didn't, rather what she did was.
She tried all over again and again and in 1997 she just broke every damn record that ever existed.
She was accepted by the 13th publisher and that was historical. It was a hell of a beautiful time and life just changed for her forever. J.K. Rowling's "Harry Potter and the Philosopher's Stone" hit the market and this changed the world of stories forever and ever. Her hard work paid dividends and she was showered with love from around the world. That's the joy of being a good person. Rowling went through anything and everything but she never stepped back she never ever gave up and fought like a brave soldier and therefore she succeeded in the long run.

She kept going and years later she became the first author to be a billionaire. That was historical. From being a broke to a billionaire. In 2007 Rowling made a record when her book Harry Potter the seventh and final version of the series became the fastest selling book and 11 million copies were sold in just 24 hours. Thus she

never gave up and kept succeeding slowly and slowly and eventually she changed the world of children's stories forever.
That is why I gave such a unusual title to this chapter. This chapter was really special for me and also for you all.
"The subtle art of just going on and on and on and on .... "
In the words of the late Charlie Liton "If you've got God, you got a friend and that friend is you".

Chapter 24: Find a remedy

"Whether you think you can or you think you can't in both ways you're correct"

-   Henry Ford

"Don't find a fault find a remedy".
Do you really know who said this and why?
Can you just guess the name of this person?
If you can then.
Then you're a very, very smart person.
Yup really, you're an intelligent person and one in a million.
Although we all are unique in some way or the other but if you
know the above answer then you're a genius and that too a
freaking crazy genius.

So let's end this guessing game and let's know who this person
was. Just one more thing and we will definitely move forward. So
we all know who is the father of automobile industry. Actually it's
just an accident that we all know that Henry Ford is the father of
automobile industry rather it's not him.
Actually its Karl Benz. That is what only few of us know.
That's the bottomline.
Oh ohoooooo............
We all know the name its Henry Ford. So let's continue the story.
Ford has always been one of the greatest innovators, mechanic,
scientist, racer, dreamer and entrepreneur and the list goes on
and on. It's a huge list and this is how we all know Henry Ford.

Ford was an exceptional person and was much advanced than the other entrepreneurs of his time. He is the only person who was also admired and liked by Adolf Hitler and he called him an inspiration and "a real inspiration".
Ford has an awesome life concept.
How?
How can I say that?
Ok.
Henry Ford knew when to just keep aside a plan and when to bring back that same plan back to the table. It happens with all of us.
Isn't it?
We all have dreams and ideals and aspirations but due to some reasons we all are forced to just put aside our plans and that is very difficult.
Really, really difficult.
I also had to go through the same thing phase and I did and I had to just ignore and postpone some of my works.
So its quite normal.
But the magic is that when you bring that same plan back to the table and work on it and fail in it and again and again and again and finally you succeed in it. It's a blessing and also a beautiful feeling.
I'm writing this book and I don't know whether it will reach its destination or not. I don't know whether you all my readers will like it or not.
I don't know whether or not I'll be the same person once this book is out in the market. I've invested a huge amount of time in this dream project of mine.
I don't know whether or not people will accept our book because in a world where only famous writers are accepted its difficult for new people to put a good show that's the harsh truth.
I know that.
But one thing that I know is that I'm doing my job. I'm writing this book and I plan that this will reach the masses and my message and my idea and perspective on business and bonding will be

liked and accepted by you all.
I believe this and this is what my job is and I'm good with this.

Let's conclude with this " Whether you think you can or you think you can't, in both ways you're correct". - Henry Ford.

Chapter 25: Just for you only

"There's a way to do it better, find it"

-   Thomas Edison

Henry Ford was one of a kind you can never ever compare with anyone else. The only person in history who has the record of keeping Thomas Edison's last breathe in a test tube which has been preserved as an artifact in Henry Ford Museum.

If you know how to bond and network and make life long relationships, then you gotta a huge skill under your belt and I therefore think you're the lucky person and you are part of 1% who are responsible for the rest 99%.

I hope you understand.

Don't you?

I hope you do understand.

Yes.

I know that.

Ford was a watch mechanic and this started of when his father got him a pocketwatch which was really, really rare thing at that time so this rare gift of Ford had a great influence on his career and he learnt how to repair watches and became an expert in it. He helped his friends by repairing their pocket watches and acquired the title of an exceptionally excellent "watch mechanic". The ability to bond, he used this skill of repairing watches and this proved to be a game changer for him.

Ford made his first mechanical car in 1878 at a tender age of 17 and this opened the doors of opportunities for him.

It was a brilliant move and took him to the next level.

The next level of excellence.

The beginning was so exciting that things were getting better and better and bigger and bigger for Ford.

Ford had a clear vision and it was to make cars cheaper in price not in quality. Cars were too expensive in America at that time, probably in 19th century and only the rich class could afford to purchase cars and this was quite unfair and unlikely for a person

like Ford. He being a part of middle class family had to do something for the masses.
So he did something.
So let's do it in this way.
Two events, two stories, two incidents that changed the history of automobile industry and these events would go down in history books as one of the most important events of 19th century.
So here we go.
Ford was recruited as the Chief Operating Engineer of Thomas Edison Project and his job was to light the whole city in the evening.
Yeah......
Sounds interesting.
Yes, it is quite interesting and unique job.
You are in charge of lighting up the city everyday, and your job will make it possible for the people to travel in the evening because street lights are also a part of lighting the city.
This too inspired him in many, many ways.
But he was too long term focused. So he thought of masses and he did this.
Ford is accredited to mass production and this changed the world economy forever. So Ford thought of making affordable cars so that the middle class could afford that too. From $800 to $250 this was the drastic price change. He planned to make cars that were so affordable that even the normal people like middle class could also afford that.
This was a historic move and had two simple results and they were.
1. The mass production formula was a hit and therefore it increased the demand for affordable cars in the market. Now cars were not confined to the yards of rich only. Now the masses had a fair amount of authority to purchase cars.
This was beautiful for the economy as well as for Ford.
2. The mass production plan just increased the employment rate and labours were in hell of a high demand.
The level of employment rose and this was the second biggest

benefit.

Henry Ford hired the labourers at double cost that means if they were given a $100 a day now Ford gave them $200 a day and this attracted all the labour talent towards Ford Motors.

That is why Henry Ford was different.

That is why Ford was the leader of masses.

Ford proved that customer's welfare was the key to success in the modern market.

It showed that bonds were greater than business in all times.

This part was a unique in itself. So why not end this one in a unique way.

You might say.

Why not?

So here's it.

"If you feed your fear your faith will die, and if you feed your faith your fear will die".

Ford feeded his faith so his fear died.

Forget your fears and look forward to your faith

Chapter 26: It's fun to do the impossible

"It always seems impossible until its done"

-   Nelson Mandela

"When you're curious you find lots of interesting things to do".
Isn't that applicable in real world?
What are your thoughts on it?
Isn't it great to look for the impossible?
Isn't it good to think that we can make the impossible a possibility some day?
What's your opinion?
What do you think?
Can you achieve the impossible?
Is that your intention in the near future?
If yes, then this part and this book is for you.
In this part I'll be taking you to another journey and with lots of twists and turns and ups and downs and you'll feel as if you're really on a roller coaster which is going down the track and again towards the top of it. It will really blow you up so be attentive and get ready.
It was exactly a century ago when one of the greatest innovators and dreamers of world history was born and this person would become the most famous Academy award winner and would create something that would be admired and loved for generations to come. This personality was born in 1901 and would face the two world wars and also the Great Depression of 1930.
He is none other than the one who made a mouse so famous that it would become one of the greatest creations of animation and children's stories. So any idea who this person is?
Any guesses?
Any clue?
Yup.
I know you all know this man.
He is none other than ....
Walt Disney.
The creator and the soul of Disneyland and more correctly the Mickey Mouse.
The most loved creature and even I love that freaking creature, we all love him.
Don't we?

That's the beauty of Disneyland and the creativity of Walt Disney. This part will be concerned with the person who created Disneyland and the only person who won the Oscars 22 times an all time record.
So let's get into the next chapter.

"All our dreams can come true, if we have the courage to persue them". - Walt Disney.

Chapter 27: It all started with the mouse

"If you can dream it, you can do it"

- Walt Disney

Walt Disney the most innovative person who made a mouse a superstar just like that. It proved that no matter how weird and unusual a thing may look like it will change the world one day only because there was a believe and faith behind the making.
Walt made a mouse a superstar because he saw innovation and creativity in it. It's a very old proverb that only "a goldsmith will be able to identify a diamond".

In our case, Walt was the goldsmith and the mouse, the Mickey Mouse was the diamond. The rarest one in the whole world. So let's look more into Walt Disney's creation and struggles.
Walt Disney was born on 5th of December in 1901 in Chicago and he was the fourth of the five children. His family moved to a farm in Marceline, Missouri when he was four.

Life was not easy and comfortable for him but he was encouraged to draw and this inspiration came from a neighbour, who was a retired doctor and his aunt. In 1910 his father sold the farm and the following year the family relocated to Kansas City.

His father purchased a newspaper route there and for the next six years Walt helped his father to deliver newspapers before and after schools and during weekends.

Later, things were quite normal yet tough for the young artist. Walt was quite inattentive while he was in school yet his love for drawing and art was growing as the days passed and this would become the thing, that would help him in future.
Disney worked as an ambulance driver for Red Cross Ambulance Corps during World War 1 where he forged his certificate to become 17 while he was just 16 because 17 was the minimum age requirement for working as the ambulance driver. He was discharged in 1919.
Disney moved to Kansas City to become a newspaper cartoonist, so you see newspaper always had a huge role in his life and career.
From distributing newspapers to being a cartoonist, but this was just the beginning. The beginning of the new era. In 1922 he started a film studio call Laugh-O- Gram and was bankrupt by 1923. Success was not that easy and never has been.
But what's there is the hope and the faith and trust in your idea. That's what's required.
Walt opened another studio called Disney Brothers Studio in 1923 with his older sibling Roy in Hollywood.
After producing a lot of films he finally got the breakthrough with Oswald the Lucky Rabbit in 1927. But unfortunately he lost the rights of the show and had a huge dispute with the employees.
Then came the legendary Mortimer Mouse. Walt dubbed the character and was the voice of Mortimer Mouse for several years. Ok.....
By the way Mortimer Mouse is our very beloved Mickey Mouse.
So Mickey made the debut in 1928 in a short film called Streamboat Willie and very quickly the rodent became so famous

that fan clubs were made for this so called "Mickey Mouse".
That was a huge success.

This is what Walt Disney said "I never want Disneyland to be
complete it should grow and develop as much as possible and
should keep on expanding till creativity exists in this world".
The ability to bond with people, with your dreams and with the
destiny and with the belief is what makes Walt Disney one of a
kind.

This is what made Walt Disney different, creative, innovative and
a brilliant entrepreneur and a world leader.
The leader who changed the world with a simple rodent, the
Mickey Mouse. Today, we have 12 Disneyland across the globe
and it was only been possible because of the bonding with the
dreams.
Walt had a beautiful bond with his dreams and believe and this is
what made Disney, The Walt Disney.
I hope we never lose sight of one thing - that it was all started by a
mouse.

Chapter 28: Compassion in life

"World peace begins with inner peace"

-   Dalai Lama

"There are two days in a year when nothing can be done, the first is yesterday and the next is tomorrow, today is the only day to love, believe, do and mostly
live".   - Dalai Lama

So, we are almost closing this journey and we are running towards the end line. So, I thought of ending this beautiful journey with someone whom the world calls the ocean of compassion, the ocean of wisdom. The ocean of peace and knowledge. There are lots and lots of things which can be said about Dalai Lama but let's look at something different and new. Happiness is not an option rather it's a compulsion. This is what His Holiness The 14th Dalai Lama has been preaching, teaching, and practicing throughout his life. The art of being peaceful, the art of being happy, the art of being humble, the art of being natural, and the art of loving the entire world irrespective of the conditions this is what we will include in this part.

The art of bonding with people from various countries, continents, and religions and regions this is what makes him different from the rest of the world.

So, in the next chapter we will look into the journey of the life of the ocean of wisdom.

Therefore, I think we need to end this one with a good thought and that to from Dalai Lama and here it is.

"My religion is very simple. My religion is kindness".

Chapter 29: Ocean of bonding and calmness

"Sometimes the questions are complicated and the answers are simple"

-   Dr. Seuss

"If you think you are too small for something then try to sleep in dark with mosquitos".

Dalai Lama was born in 1935 and at the age of 2, he was identified as the reincarnation of the 13th Dalai Lama. Although his life has been full of struggles yet he loved every moment of it and that is what we call compassion and wisdom. Lhamo Dhondup the name that was given to him when he was born in 1935 in Taktser in northeastern Tibet in the family of peasant

They were very poor but this child was born to change the world and to lead the world too.

He became a monk when he was 6 and was named as Tensin Gyatso. He took the control of Tibet when he was 4 and this was too unique and one of a kind in itself. Dalai Lama lived in the thousand-year-old Potala Palace before the Chinese Army crushed the uprising in Tibet in 1959. Ever since then he has been struggling to get his homeland back for the Buddhist monks. He has been living as a refugee in India since 1959 with 10000 other monks but still, that hope, that faith, and the trust always exists and will continue to exist forever and ever. That is what we call patience, determination, and compassion towards the whole world.

He was awarded the NOBEL PEACE PRIZE in 1989 for his works that advocated to free Tibet from China only and only through nonviolent means. He is also very passionate about repairing watches, meditation, and gardening. He shares a beautiful bond with our nature and that is why he is so calm and peaceful. If you connect with nature you connect with God.

He also has a deep interest in science and technology. Once he said that Buddhism and science are very much related and if science proves anything in Buddhism that is wrong then it needs to change. Science and Buddhism share a search for truth and reality.

He will be happy to return to Tibet if no conditions are applied to him. Therefore, he has been attacked a lot of times and remains in high security.

The art of happiness and spreading love are some of his basic teachings and beliefs. So, we learn a lot from this person and I conclude with one of his sayings.

World peace begins with inner peace.

SECTION 4: THINK DIFFERENT

"You have to dream before, dreams come true"

-   Dr A.P.J. Abdul Kalam

Chapter 30: Age Bond Graph

"Age is just an issue of mind over matter, if you don't mind it does'nt matters"

-   Mark Twain

"You are never too young to change the world".
The more you bond the more opportunities you create for yourself
and the more you get in the right track. The more you bond the
more is the chance that you might be able to migrate from one job
to another.
Age is just a number and hence it should never ever effect your
bonding opportunities but fortunately or unfortunately it does and
therefore most of the people do suffer from this problem.

Do you remember when we were a year or a two old, we never
hesitated to ask something.
Same applies for people who are in their late 50's or early 60's
and the people older than that. They never hesitate to bond
likewise, they never have any problem to talk to a stranger or to
relate with them in some way or the other.
That's the catch and that's the fact of the matter.
Age is just a digit.
Nothing else.
If you think age will hinder your progress then my dear reader's
you're wrong. Rather quite incorrect and out of the track.
For instance kids under 16 years of age tend to bond more and
they often develop healthy bonds with everyone irrespective of
situation. On the other hand people who are quite aged might be
between 60's and 70's or people older than that also bond very,
very well. That's weird but it actually works. Young people and
aging young people both bond with a special motive and that
motive is to make life long relationships.
"We make a living by what we get, and we make a life by what we
give". Winston Churchill.
But the fact is this doesn't happens in case of people who are in
their early 20's, 30's, 40's and late 40's they all have a problem
with bonding with someone new whose a stranger to them. The
main factors that effect these people's ability to make a new
relationship in business are as follows:-
1. Ego
2. Shyness

3. Inflexibility
4. Hesitancy
5. Pessimistic attitude
6. Lack of transparency
7. Trust and Faith issues.
8. The list goes on and on and on...................

The graph above shows the same thing. I really don't have any idea why age is a bar while we bond or when we try to build more and more personal and professional relationships. Age is just that number that increases with the passing of every moment and every moment gives you that experience that is worth life long.

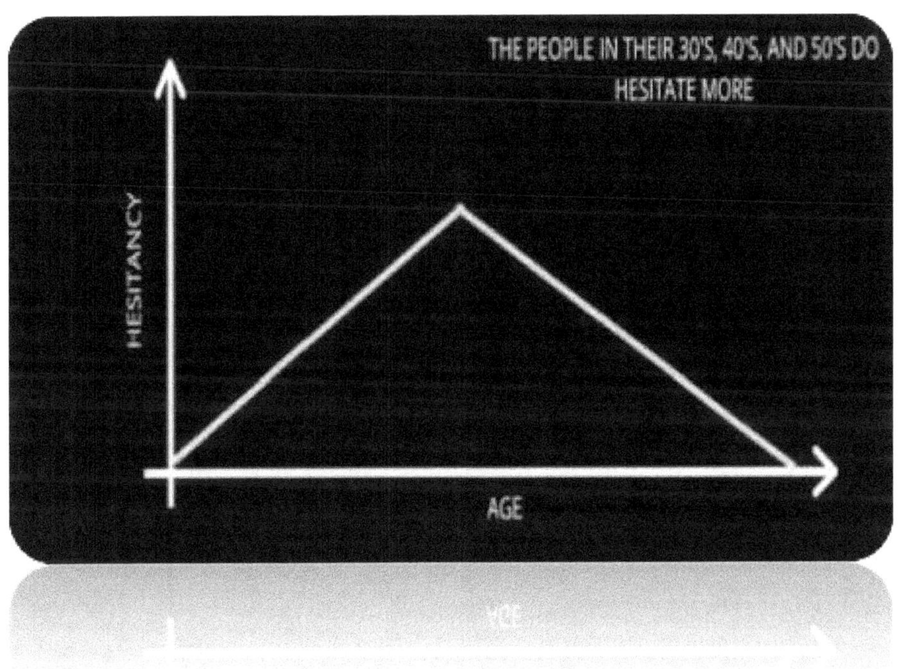

These factors are the greatest hindrances that people in the above age groups face in their daily lives. Its been a great way and hence these factors do effect all businesses some way or the other.

Don't let these factors effect you in any way. If you do, then forget about bonding and keep this book in your store room.

Just forget about the bonding schemes and loose this book somewhere and sometime and somehow.

It's quite weird to say but I analysed and I found something quite interesting and unique.

This will blow you up as it did blow me up when I got such brilliant results. So here's what I found. The results will shake you up so take a seat and read this slowly and slowly.

Slow and steady wins the race.

So I found that the 2 age groups I explained earlier, the younger generation and the little older generation are the ones who bond very quickly and they have that believe that we all are made to live and grow together so here's my conclusion on this:-

1. They don't care what people think about them.

2. They love everything from nature to birds to clothing and accessories.

3. They live life according to days. Like everyday is a new day and will bring lots of experiences in their lives.

4. They think and believe that we live only once and once.

5. They are the ones who prove the Steve Jobs statement correct." The people who are crazy enough to think that they can change the world are the ones who do".

That's how I conclude my study and one short statement for you all.

Either put up or shut up. I'm sorry for these harsh words but sometimes a bitter medicine is required to cure us.

Isn't it?

Am I saying something out of the box.

No.........not at all.

It's the part and parcel of your business. Ask and you shall receive. Think and you're half way through.

Apply the method and change your own world.

Chapter 31: THE REBT

"Either create your future or let it create you"

-   Manas Roy

"If you're not making mistakes you're not trying something new". - Elon Musk.
Why did I start with this quote?
Why?
Why?
Why?
There are numerous reasons but I have a gift for you all.
I love giving you all these gifts and I love the look of amazement on your faces. Therefore I wondered how can I gift you something and I thought of this.

Long ago I took a course and I loved it. Coincidentally, that same course came with me along the way and I finally thought of adding the same in this book. Finally I thought of this and I added that study in the book.
REBT. Rational Emotive Behavior Theory. This will look like something scientific and philosophical but I tell you it's not. Believe me on this when I tell you this. Its just another way to bond with people. I'll not expand this too much but I'll keep it straight and short.
Just think about it, you were driving a car and suddenly you were overtaken by a taxi or a cab. Just think it in this way. The cab overtakes your car an you're frustrated and devastated by this incident. Now what you thought was why not just take the frustrations out on that cab driver. So you got out of the car and ..... and let's move to the next paragraph.
You got out of your car and you're screaming and howling on the driver and the driver is also screaming and shouting on you and this creates a huge commotion and suddenly the person who was in the cab comes out and as he tries to say something to you.
But you start shouting on that person too and it's a holy hell of situation.
You were on the way to meet with your future client and finally after a lot of trouble you reached your destination and you're about to meet your customers and you opened the door.
And ....

your client but now.

What?
You lost that client once and for all. Not only you lost that client
but you lost atleast a dozens of future clients and that's only
because you suffered from anger problems.
This is what I call REBT. GIVE ME 5 MINUTES AND I'LL MAKE
THINGS CRYSTAL CLEAR FOR YOU.
You changed your thoughts into your actions and your actions
gave you your results.
Thoughts ~ Actions ~ Results.

I hope you do understand this but the fact is you can use REBT to
the best of your advantage like if you would've kept yourself in
control you would've never been angry and hence you would
never have lost your client and further dozens of clients in the
near future.
That's nothing but the reaction to your actions.
Either you respond or you react.
That's the question.
Someone very intellectual said this to me that " Every action has
an equal and opposite reaction".

This is what I call this REBT and I think you'll use it in a positive way all the time. See you in the next chapter.

Chapter 32: The BFS of our Life

"Be the change you want to see in the world"

-   M.K. Gandhi

The book, I hope is entertaining you so far and by the way do you remember in the earlier parts of this book I showed you all what is our BBC concept.
Yeah
Remember that.
I hope you still remember a few bits and bites and tits and tats of that concept.
If you're thinking that I'm gonna give you a revision of that part then let me tell you all.
Hell no...............

I'm not a primary school teacher who has the patience and time to repeat things over and over and over again.

Love to all teachers around the world.

This chapter is about one more of such practical concepts that you can fairly apply to change your concepts of bonds and this concept will help you to bonds well. I showed you what are bonds. I showed you who used and uses bonds from top entrepreneurs to investors to dreamers to innovators to artists and people from various other professions. It's time to show you all how to bond and the various methods of bonding in 2020 and even after this year.
Here's the punch.
BFS or the Background Facts and Stories is a beautiful and beautiful lesson that life taught me in the several years of my public speaking career. See I never told you all this but I saved it for the future.
I believe that "Save the best for the future".
I hope you got the catch.
Did you?
Oh yeah......
Yes you did get the point.
The BFS is a simple formula that the most influential and famous people of the world use while they are bonding with huge groups

of people might be tens and thousands of people at the same time. So let's jump into the simple thing.

B. F. S.

B = BACKGROUND. By background I mean the background of a person whom you're ready to bond with. "Someone's background might be your foreground". So before you bond with a person you need to know atleast something about them.

Why?

The reason is you can never test the depth of water without getting into it. You need to know who the person is. What is he known for. And the most important why am I gonna bond with this person?

To know all this you need to know about the person. So how is that possible. Search on LinkedIn, YouTube, Facebook, Instagram and Twitter and if possible.

Let me tell you if possible just go to Amazon and search for their name and if you find a book or two in that person's name then mark that point.

Think about it you're meeting someone for coffee and you know what this person is all about and what he does. Just start the conversation with some off topics like sports, just know what sports are they interested in and break the ice with that topic.

I know you might be thinking this author is a little crazy. But believe me when I say this to you just try this and you'll praise me always. Just believe me.

Follow this quote please "RELATIONS ARE MORE IMPORTANT THAN PRODUCT KNOWLEDGE AT ALL TIMES". This is what only some of people including you understand. Use it and let's move to the next one.

F = facts. The facts are nothing that special but the tips and little events that happen to you when you bond. Think about it once you were in for a coffee with the CEO of Apple or Hubspot or some other company as you like it and you forgot your wallet. Think about it how funny and pathetic it would've been.

But share these things with the person whom you're meeting for some reason. You'll see the magic. People will love your way because you're friendly and quite simple in terms of communicating with them. Just apply it and see the results.

S = Stories. I think the best way to explain something to someone that is quite complex is to narrate a related story and make things easier and easier for all.

Albert Einstein, my favourite scientist once said " If you can't teach something to a 6 year old then probably you never understood it yourself".

If you wanna control any conversation just start a story. People love stories irrespective of the situation. Just narrate and see what happens. When you include yourself in any of your stories people start believing you and that's where you get the edge over others.

So I hope that you will use this simple yet effective formula in the best way possible and to most of your advantage.

Just let me know if you get any success from this formula.

"Sometimes the heart sees what's invisible to the eye". Jackson Jr.

I hope you will learn something new everyday from now on.

I hope you loved it. See you in the next chapter.

Chapter 33 : Look for the negatives first

"One book, one pen, one child and one teacher can change the world"

-   Malala Yousafzai

"A wise man will make more opportunities than he finds".

This is very true for our case and our book and do you all remember what I promised you all in the beginning of the book. I hope you do remember but if not let me remind you all. This is not a book designed in the form of book, it is designed to give you all a movie like experience and this experience will be a memorable one forever and I promise you'll carry something with you forever. So, I hope you realized.

We all hate negativity, don't we?

We all have different problems with negative people, don't we?

But there's something different than what meets to the eye. Things are not that bad and disgraceful as it seems to be. While we are on the way to bond with people, we need to remember this little concept. The look for negative concept.

You might be wondering what on earth is this now. It's a brilliant way to analyze people and specially when you're bonding with new people and that's awesome and I love it. I'm not telling this to brag upon you rather to impress upon you the fact that I have a very unique gift that I was born with and it's that I can read people like a book and I read their minds through their eyes and I love it. I love it when people literally hesitate to make eye contact and it's the biggest proof that the person is lying and betraying you and don't trust that person. Moving on, so when you know that you're trying to connect with a person who can benefit you in every way possible don't, don't, don't go with the flow you will drown eventually.

Why?

Why not?

There are tons and tons of reasons to look for and hence I will be showing some to you.

If you look for the positives too much you will force yourself to ignore the negatives and it will be not that good for you or for your company and therefore, I think you need to know this very well enough and here we go: -

If you are meeting the top CEO of any company you need to find out the negative effects of it.
What are the ill effects or disadvantages of meeting this man and you will be able to get a good view of what I'm telling you? You already know the positive points and you will always be benefited by it but what we forget is what about the negative effects.
This will be a changing factor and most of us ignore this. Due to this mistake we fall in such a situation where we fall in a huge trouble and this is an unignorable situation.

Take my advice and read this as a suggestion and you will never see yourself in trouble.

Look at the negative sides first and try to convert those negative points as opportunities and future chances and see how your career changes once and for all.

Change your view and see how the world changes for you. The more you adapt to the situations the more are the doors of opportunities going to open for you.
At last keep the merits of bonding in your pocket and look for the demerits.

Identify them.

Analyze them and try and keep trying to change the negatives to the positives once and for all. This will really help you in the long run.

Finally, "Be the change you want to see in the world". – Mahatma Gandhi

<u>C</u><u>ONCLUSION</u>

"The two most important days in your life are, the day you are born and the day you find out why."

-   Mark Twain

Thank you for your time and dedication.

I hope you loved this book and you learnt something new and different. I humbly believe that we learn something new everyday and this is your chance.

Be the one who can change the world anytime, anywhere, and at any place.

God bless you all forever.

I hope to see you all very soon.

Feel free to connect with me and keep bonding.

Just change the lens through which you see the world and then you will see the difference in your life.

Thank you.

Manas Roy:)